# Wrecks of American Warships

**James P. Delgado**

*Watts* LIBRARY

**Franklin Watts**
A Division of Grolier Publishing
New York • London • Hong Kong • Sydney
Danbury, Connecticut

*The author would like to thank his wife, Ann Goodhart, William S. Dudley, Robert Neyland, Paul F. Johnston, Art Cohn, Warren Reiss, Sheli Smith, Donald G. Shomette, George Belcher, John Broadwater, William N. Still Jr., Chris Amer, Max Guerout, Richard Lawrence, Roger Smith, Daniel J. Lenihan, Larry Murphy, Larry Nordby, and Jerry Livingston.*

**Note to readers:** Definitions for words in **bold** can be found in the Glossary at the back of this book.

Photographs ©: Corbis-Bettmann: 52, 53, 46, 47 (Hulton-Deutsch Collection), 36 (UPI) : 12, 42, 43; Courtesy of Donald Shomette, Cultural Resource Management, Dunkirk, MD: 29; Cynthia Orr: 21 (D. Switzer); James P. Delgado: 6, 7, 11, 12; Lake Champlain Maritime Museum: 17; Liaison Agency, Inc.: 26 (J. Bourg), 3 bottom, 48 (Hulton Getty), 4, 5; Maine State Museum: 24, 25; National Park Service, Submerged Cultural Resources Unit, Santa Fe, NM: 8, 9, 34, 35, 39, 40 (John D. Brooks), 3 top, 30, 32, 50; North Wind Picture Archives: 14; Robert Cole: 23; Smithsonian Institution, Washington, DC: 15, 16; Superstock, Inc.: 18; The Museum of the Confederacy, Richmond, VA.: 41 (Katherine Wetzel).

Visit Franklin Watts on the Internet at:
http://publishing.grolier.com

**Library of Congress Cataloging-in-Publication Data**

Delgado, James P.
    Wrecks of American warships / James P. Delgado.
        p.     cm.— (Watts Library)
    Includes bibliographical references and index.
    Summary : Examines the excavations of sunken American Navy warships from the Revolutionary War to World War II and discusses what they tell us about life on board these vessels.
    ISBN: 0-531-20376-X (lib. bdg.)        0-531-16486-1 (pbk.)
    1. Warships—United States Juvenile literature. 2. Shipwrecks—United States Juvenile literature. 3. Underwater archaeology—United States Juvenile literature. 4. Excavations (Archaeology)—United States Juvenile literature. 5. United States—Antiquities Juvenile literature. [1. Warships—History. 2. Shipwrecks. 3. Underwater archaeology.] I. Title. II. Series.
VA55.D45  2000
910.4'52'0973—dc21

                                                    99-25426
                                                   CIP

# Contents

Introduction
**Dive, Dive!** 5

Chapter One
**Exploring Lost Warships** 9

Chapter Two
**The Beginnings of the U.S. Navy** 13

Chapter Three
**A Great Disaster** 19

Chapter Four
**The War of 1812** 27

Chapter Five
**A Cursed Ship** 31

Chapter Six
**The Civil War** 37

Chapter Seven
**The Rise of the Modern Navy** 43

Chapter Eight
**World War II** 49

54 **Glossary**

57 **To Find Out More**

60 **A Note on Sources**

61 **Index**

*The USS Arizona Memorial in Pearl Harbor, Hawaii, is built over the sunken wreck.*

# Dive, Dive!

It was 1988, and I was standing on the dock at the USS *Arizona* Memorial at Pearl Harbor, Hawaii. After ten years of diving on shipwrecks around the world, I was about to jump into the dark, oily waters that surround this famous U.S. battleship. The sinking of the *Arizona* on the morning of December 7, 1941, was one of the acts that pushed the United States into World War II. Since then, the *Arizona* had rested on the bottom, with the bodies of more than 1,000 crew members still inside.

Diving on the *Arizona* was like entering a tomb. Warships are not like other shipwrecks. They are reminders of bravery, fierce battles, the price of victory, and the bitterness of defeat.

For most of my career as an underwater **archaeologist**, I have dived on lost warships. They include the USS *Arizona*, the U.S. **brig** *Somers*, and the ships sunk by the atomic bomb at Bikini island in the Pacific Ocean. I also worked on the USS

*An archaeological search in Pearl Harbor*

*Monitor* project for a year and visited nearly every historic warship that has been preserved in a museum. I have seen battleships, aircraft carriers, destroyers, and **men-of-war** by the light of day and in the darkness of the deep.

I have also worked with other archaeologists who have studied warships. These scientists have studied ancient battleships rowed by men, huge wooden warships from early battles when cannons battered ships into wrecks, and other wrecks from nearly every period of U.S. history. Because of archaeology, we know how these ships looked, how the crews lived aboard them, and how the crews died.

During World War II, submariners went into action with the command "dive, dive!" It's our turn now. Let's dive deep into the ocean, and into the past.

—James P. Delgado

*Many American warships sank during battle. This is the wheel of the CSS Alabama, which went down in 1864.*

# Chapter One

# Exploring Lost Warships

The sea covers most of the earth. Since ancient times, people have built ships to cross the ocean, fish and hunt on the ocean, and fight on the ocean. Many of these ships now lie on the bottom of the sea or in lakes and rivers.

For more than 200 years, the people of the United States have seen the sea as a barrier to enemies in distant lands. They built a navy with ships to defend the nation. The sea has been an important battlefield for the United States, and hundreds of U.S. Navy ships lie on the ocean floor. These warships date from the beginning of the navy. They include boats rowed with oars into battle, sailing ships, iron-hulled steamships, **submarines**, battleships, and aircraft carriers. They include ships sunk in storms after running into reefs or rocks, and ships felled in battle by cannonballs, shells from huge guns, torpedoes, and bombs. Underwater archaeologists have discovered and studied hundreds of sunken U.S. warships around the world.

Many warships fought in battles to protect our freedom. Some of these ships, such as the famous sailing ship USS *Constitution* ("Old Ironsides") in Boston, Massachusetts, are preserved today as museum ships. Many more lie wrecked. Some, such as the CSS *H. L. Hunley* and the USS *Arizona*, are war graves that rest where they sank, their crews buried with them underwater. Most are still owned by the U.S. Navy and protected by law from being **pilfered** or **salvaged**. All of them are windows to the past.

*A replica of the Confederate submarine* H. L. Hunley

*The Battle of Lexington took place in 1775.*

# Chapter Two

# The Beginnings of the U.S. Navy

The Revolutionary War began in 1775 when British troops and colonial farmers exchanged shots in Lexington, Massachusetts. Some Revolutionary War battles were fought on the water. Those battles marked the beginning of the U.S. Navy.

The oldest American warship that archaeologists have studied is the **gunboat** *Philadelphia*. It was one of eight gunboats

*American general
Benedict Arnold*

**What Is a
Gunboat?**

A gunboat was a flat-bottomed boat that carried cannons. The boat had a mast and a sail, but when a gunboat had to move quickly, the crew would row with oars.

built for American general Benedict Arnold in the summer of 1776. Arnold needed the gunboats to stop a British fleet from sailing down Lake Champlain and seizing control of the lake and the Hudson River in New York. Traveling on lakes and rivers was one of the best ways to move men and equipment, and Arnold wanted to keep this travel route from the British.

Arnold's fleet of gunboats was built quickly. When it went into battle, soldiers joined the crews because there were not enough sailors. On October 11, 1776, Arnold and his small fleet met twenty-nine British ships. Arnold's fleet was pushed back. Two ships—the *Philadelphia* and the schooner *Royal Savage*—sank. The next day, the British destroyed most of Arnold's remaining ships. Because winter was coming, the British pulled back, and the Americans had the winter to build up their forces.

## Bringing up the *Philadelphia*

In 1935, Colonel Lorenzo F. Hagglund, a New York diver and salvage engineer, discovered the wreck of the *Philadelphia* in 54 feet (16 meters) of water. The cold, fresh waters of Lake Champlain had preserved the ship. With no sea creatures to eat the wood and the cold acting like a refrigerator, the ship was solid after almost 150 years.

Colonel Hagglund pumped out the water, put the *Philadelphia* on a barge, and sailed it around the lake for tourists to visit. In 1961, the gunboat was given to the Smithsonian Institution in Washington, D.C.

## The *Philadelphia* Discoveries

Archaeologists and historians carefully studied the *Philadelphia*. Because the gunboat was built without plans, no one knew what it looked like. Researchers learned that it was built like a **gondola**, a flat-bottomed cargo boat. The *Philadelphia*, however, was stronger than a typical gondola, with larger timbers to carry heavy cannons and guns.

At the time of the Revolutionary War, guns were in short supply and older ones were often reused. Archaeologists discovered that the guns aboard the *Philadelphia* had been between seventy-five and one hundred years old in 1776. They also discovered that the navy had painted the gunboat with tar, probably because they had no paint.

The *Philadelphia*'s crew sat on large benches to row the gunboat into battle. They were protected by large bundles of twigs and saplings that were tied together along the sides of the boat. These bundles were known as **fascines**. The fascines

*The oldest American man-of-war in existence is the* Philadelphia.

### A Fascine in Your Pocket!

If you look closely at the eagle on the back of a U.S. quarter, you can see a fascine clutched in the eagle's talons.

## Artifacts from the *Philadelphia*

The *Philadelphia* crew left behind many of their things, including these coins. Archaeologists call these items *artifacts*. Artifacts tell how the crew lived, ate, and fought. Shoes and buckles show that the men wore their own clothing instead of uniforms. Spoons and a ceramic cup show that the crew brought items from home. And gunflints, bayonets, and buckshot show that many of the sailors carried and used their own weapons. Crew members made use of their weapons to exchange shots if another ship got close. Sometimes, in an effort to seize an enemy ship, they would board the ship and fight hand to hand.

did not save the ship, however. A cannonball fired by a British gun was found in the broken planks of the bow. The *Philadelphia* sank about an hour after it was hit, giving the crew time to escape.

In 1989, the Lake Champlain Maritime Museum built a full-size copy of the *Philadelphia*. They built the boat to see exactly how the *Philadelphia* worked on the water. In 1996, they discovered another sunken gunboat—perfectly preserved and very similar to the *Philadelphia*. They will continue to study the wreck for several years to add to our knowledge of early American warships.

*The* Philadelphia II *is a full-sized copy of the original gunboat.*

British men-of-war
on the open sea

# Chapter Three

# A Great Disaster

Early in the Revolutionary War, the colonies prepared for war at sea. The British Royal Navy was the most powerful navy in the world. The thirteen colonies built warships and used **privateers**, which were vessels owned by private citizens. Archaeologists discovered and **excavated** one of these ships in 1972.

## The Penobscot Expedition

In 1779, the largest American naval **expedition** of the Revolutionary War sailed from Boston, Massachusetts, to Penobscot Bay in Maine. Fifty-five ships carrying nearly 2,000 men headed to the area to drive British forces out. They sailed into disaster.

The British had only three warships on the Penobscot River, but six more were on their way. The Americans landed and waited. When the British fleet arrived, the American troops and ships were forced to retreat. Because the British ships had blocked them, they could not sail back to sea. Most of the American ships traveled up the Penobscot River, with the British close behind. The Americans, finally trapped, set their ships on fire and sank them to avoid capture. One of the last American ships left afloat was the small brig *Defence*. But when the British spotted the *Defence* sailing into the harbor, the crew, unable to escape, set the ship on fire and rowed to shore. The *Defence* sank into the harbor.

The Penobscot expedition was one of the worst naval defeats in American history. Five hundred men were killed and forty-two ships were lost. Although people discovered cannons from the lost fleet, no one knew much about what the ships looked like or what life was like onboard—until 1972, when students from the Maine Maritime Academy discovered

## Pirate Ships

Privateers usually did not do battle with warships. Instead, they preyed on unarmed enemy merchant ships. Privateers have been called "pirate ships," which plundered with the permission of their government. The practice of using privateers is no longer accepted, however, and modern navies do not use them.

the wreck of the *Defence* under 25 feet (8 m) of water. From 1975 to 1981 the excavation of the *Defence* was carried out by college students learning to be nautical archaeologists.

## Mapping the *Defence*

Archaeologists and students excavated and mapped the underwater wreck of the *Defence*, studied the insides of the ship, and recovered hundreds of **artifacts.** They also learned that the **magazine**, where the ship's gunpowder was stored, had been at the back end, or **stern**, of the ship. Broken and burned timbers showed that the crew had set fire to the magazine to blow up and sink the *Defence*.

*This cross section of the* Defence's *hull shows the location of artifacts.*

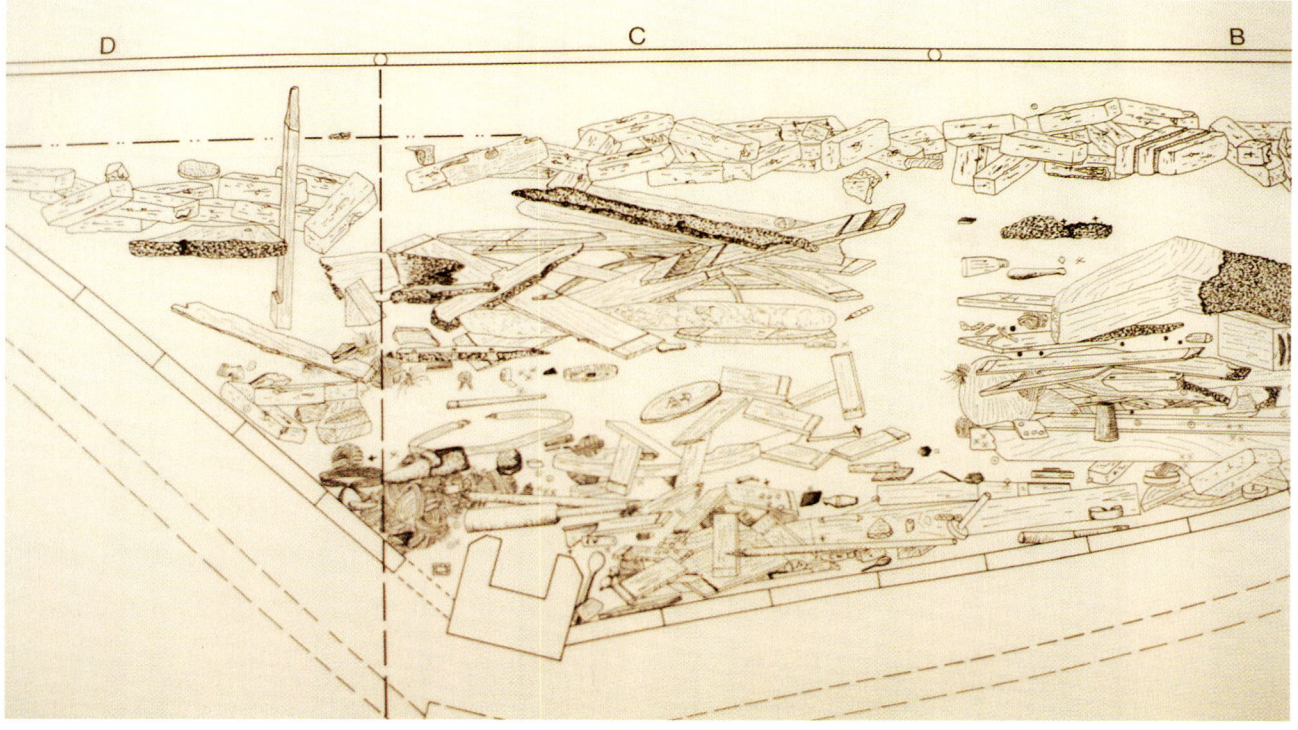

Archaeologists learned about the *Defence* by drawing a map underwater. They used Mylar—a plastic that can be written on—taped to a clipboard. An ordinary pencil writes on Mylar, even when it's wet.

## A Revolutionary War Time Capsule

After making the map, the archaeologists marked the location of every artifact they found. On the map, many artifacts lying close to one another showed where disappeared parts of the ship had been. For instance, the galley, where the crew cooked and ate their meals, was located where a large brick and copper cookstove was found.

Thousands of artifacts were brought up from the wreck. Archaeologists called it "a Revolutionary War time capsule." They found broken barrels filled with pig and cow bones and animals parts that aren't usually eaten—such as half a head. The barrels were originally packed with salt to dry out the meat and keep it from rotting. Sailors aboard the *Defence* ate this meat after it had been soaked in water to soften it.

The archaeologists found wooden plates and spoons that the crew used. They also discovered wooden tags with numbers, which at first, they thought were game pieces. Then they determined that each tag belonged to a mess, which was a group of about twelve men who ate their meals together. Each mess received a large piece of salt pork or beef, attached a wooden tag to it, and gave it to the ship's cook. He boiled it with the other messes' rations in the ship's huge stove. Once

### "Salt Horse"

Sailors hated the salted meat they were served on ships and called it "salt horse." The archaeologists who excavated the salt pork in the *Defence* could easily understand why the sailors did not want to eat it.

22

*A student archaeologist with a pewter spoon found at the **Defence** site*

*The* Defence's *crew used these wooden tags to identify their portion of "salt horse" after it was boiled to become edible.*

the meat was cooked, a mess member would take it back to the group and divide it. This system allowed the cook to serve food quickly to a large number of men.

Other artifacts from the wreck included shoes, belt buckles, and clothes. None of the men wore uniforms. One small button from a soldier's uniform, marked "USA," was found.

Either soldiers were aboard the ship or the button was a souvenir kept by one of the sailors. The archaeologists also found a clay pipe, with teeth marks on its stem.

Before the excavation of the *Defence* ended, the archaeologists completely cleared out the inside of the ship's sunken **hull**, which had been filled with mud. They were able to learn how the *Defence* had looked and how it was built. The remains of the hull showed that the *Defence* was built to sail fast, but it had been quickly constructed. Some of the work was not good. The builders of the *Defence* may have built it knowing that as a privateer the ship would not last long.

*This well-preserved leather shoe was salvaged from the mud at the* Defence *wreck.*

The archaeologists also found that the small ship was very crowded. As many as 100 men lived aboard the *Defence*. Almost all of them lived in an area 25 by 20 feet (8 by 6 m) in the middle of the ship. In this area, archaeologists found the canvas hammocks, wooden chests, and personal belongings of the sailors.

The work on the *Defence* provided some important clues about the ill-fated Penobscot expedition. In the 1990s, archaeologists began a search for more ships from this naval disaster to learn more about those times and the beginnings of the navy.

*The USS* Constitution
*fought during the War
of 1812.*

# Chapter Four

# The War of 1812

After the Revolutionary War, the navy was sold and its sailors were sent home. American ships appeared on every sea in order to trade with other countries. But because the United States had no navy to protect it, its ships were seized. Sailors were forced to worked on British warships or to become slaves of "pirates" in the Mediterranean Sea.

In 1794, Congress approved funds to build a new navy with new ships. One of those new ships was the **frigate** USS *Constitution*.

# The Chesapeake Flotilla

Britain and the United States fought in the War of 1812. Although ships such as the *Constitution* did battle at sea, most conflicts were fought close to shore or on lakes. Archaeologists have discovered the wrecks of several ships from the War of 1812. A group of wrecks known as the Chesapeake **flotilla** lies in the muddy waters of Maryland's Patuxent River.

Revolutionary War hero captain Joshua Barney commanded the flotilla, which included small gunboats and small barges that carried guns. His job was to protect the Chesapeake Bay from the British troops. Joshua Barney's flotilla drove off two British frigates in their first battle. But the British brought in more ships and chased the flotilla up the river. Cornered, Barney ordered his men to blow up their ships.

# Discovering the *Scorpion*

Archaeologists discovered the wreck of Barney's flagship, the USS *Scorpion*, in 1980. They also found the remains of some of the gunboats. Using an underwater **dredge** inside a watertight enclosure called a **cofferdam**, archaeologists cleared away the mud, which had perfectly preserved the ship and its artifacts.

The archaeologists found the surgical tools and medicines that the ship's doctor had lost. Amazingly, some of the bottles still had ointment in them. The oars, the benches the crew sat on when they rowed, weapons, a box of munitions, carpenter's tools, clothing, shoes, and a cup with the initials of the ship's cook were found. These items give us a better look at the sea battles of War of 1812 than any history book can.

## Other Wrecks from the War of 1812

Archaeologists have also discovered wrecks of other warships from the War of 1812. They studied the remains of the twenty-gun brig *Eagle* on Lake Champlain. The *Eagle* survived the war and ended its days with other ships in a backwater where they deteriorated and sank. An examination of the *Eagle* has shown that it was built quickly and cheaply. Shipbuilders took many shortcuts during its construction, thus making the *Eagle* unfit for service after the war.

Archaeologists have also surveyed two complete warships, the *Hamilton* and the *Scourge*, which sank together in a storm on Lake Ontario in 1813. Built as trading schooners, they were armed with guns and sent out to fight during the war. The guns proved too heavy, however, and when the storm struck, the ships sank. These wrecks have been visited only briefly since they lie in 300 feet (92 m) of water—too deep for scuba divers to work safely for long periods of time.

*Archaeologists believe that a member of the* Scorpion *crew cut tobacco on this large 1803 Liberty Head copper penny found at the site.*

*This tin-plated grog ration cup bearing the initials "CW" belonged to the ship's cook, Caeser Wentworth.*

*The U.S. brig* Somers *served as a floating navy school.*

# Chapter Five

# A Cursed Ship

By the end of the War of 1812, the U.S. Navy had become a growing force. Many officers had made their careers in the navy. The navy decided to train young men to become officers. It built two small, fast ships as floating schools—the *Somers* and the *Bainbridge*.

The *Somers* became one of the most notorious ships in the history of the navy. On its second voyage, the captain and his officers decided that a nineteen-year-old officer, Philip Spencer, was plotting to kill them and seize the ship. Spencer and many sailors were arrested. After a very quick trial, Spencer and two other men were hanged.

### What Is a Mutiny?

A mutiny is when sailors plot to take control—or actually seize control—of a ship.

After the mutiny, many people believed that bad luck followed the *Somers*. Sailors claimed that the ghosts of the dead men haunted the ship. The ship's doctor committed suicide. The first mate became a heavy drinker. The captain never commanded another ship, and the *Somers* was retired as a school ship.

In 1846, the United States and Mexico went to war. The United States wanted lands claimed by Mexico. The *Somers* was sent to blockade the Mexican port of Veracruz. While chasing a Mexican ship, the *Somers* was caught in a sudden storm. Heavy winds blew the ship over, and it sank instantly, drowning thirty-nine men.

*The* Somers *sank near the Mexican port of Veracruz in 1846.*

When the *Somers* went down, several warships were nearby. They launched their boats and saved many crew members, including the commander, Lieutenant Raphael Semmes. He later served as an officer in the Confederate navy during the Civil War.

## The *Somers* on the Ocean Floor

In 1986, the *Somers* wreck was discovered in 110 feet (34 m) of water. In 1990, a team of U.S. and Mexican underwater archaeologists studied the remains of the *Somers*. They found the ship lying on its side. Most of the wood had been eaten by undersea worms called **teredos**. The ship's ten cannons, anchors, stove, and other artifacts were found on the ocean floor. Everything lay exactly where it had been inside the ship, including a loaded cannon.

Divers laid out a **baseline** and measured the position of everything they found on the *Somers* wreck. They used underwater cameras to take pictures. Other divers made sketches of the wreck and took notes on Mylar. On the beach, the archaeologists used the photos, video, sketches, and notes to make a careful plan of the wreck site.

Archaeologists are still studying the wreck of the *Somers*. Sand preserved some of the bottom of the ship, allowing archaeologists to see how the ship was built. The *Somers* was a **clipper**, a fast-sailing ship with tall masts and large sails. The bottom of the hull was so narrow that a man could stand up inside it and touch both sides with his hands. In most other

### What Is a Baseline?

The line that archaeologists use to map a wreck is called a baseline. It is usually divided up in meter-long sections. All measurements made on the wreck start from the baseline.

The author and another archaeologist explore the Somers wreck.

ships of that time, it would take several men standing shoulder to shoulder to reach the sides.

The archaeologists also found that the *Somers* did not carry enough weight inside the ship to keep it from rolling over in a strong wind. The masts and sails were too tall and too big for the ship. Back then, the navy was putting new inventions and ships quickly to use. The navy learned from its mistakes and used many of the lessons it learned a few years later during the Civil War.

*The crew poses on the deck of the Monitor.*

# Chapter Six

# The Civil War

In the 1850s, the U.S. Navy experimented with powerful guns that fired exploding shells, an advancement over the old-fashioned solid cannonballs. Ships with steam engines began to replace sailing ships. When the Civil War began in 1861, all of these inventions completely changed the way wars were fought at sea.

During the Civil War, the first fight between **ironclads**—wooden ships covered with armor—took place. The fight between the U.S. ironclad *Monitor* and the Confederate ironclad *Virginia* in 1862 convinced navies to replace their old wooden ships. Both the U.S. and Confederate navies built hundreds of ironclad warships.

## Studying the Ironclad *Monitor*

Archaeologists have studied more Civil War wrecks than any other type of ship. They have dived on several U.S. and Confederate ironclads. One of them is the most famous ironclad—the USS *Monitor*. The *Monitor* was the first iron-hulled warship with a steam engine and guns inside a revolving round tower, or **turret**. Modern warships owe much of their design to the *Monitor*.

The wreck of the *Monitor* lies upside down in 240 feet (73 m) of water off the North Carolina coast. Archaeologists have studied the partly broken up ship and learned many details about how it was built. They used a powerful dredge to excavate the captain's cabin.

Life aboard the ship was difficult and uncomfortable. The steam engines and the sun shining on the iron hull made for hot working conditions. Artifacts from the captain's cabin showed that life for the officers was better. They ate fancy food and used plates, silverware, and glasses.

## A Raider Wreck

The Confederates built a small group of fast steam-powered warships called **raiders** to attack and sink merchant ships. These raiders carried the Civil War to the high seas and destroyed many American ships around the world. The most

## The *Alabama*'s Toilet

The toilet raised from the wreck of the CSS *Alabama* has many features of a modern toilet, including a round bowl that flushes. It is decorated inside with a fancy scene in blue and white.

famous raider was the CSS *Alabama*. Its commander was Raphael Semmes, who had served as captain of the *Somers* when it sank in Mexico in 1846.

Archaeologists have also discovered the wreck of the raider *Alabama*. In 1864, the U.S. warship *Kearsarge* caught the *Alabama* in the harbor of Cherbourg in France. The *Alabama* sank in more than 200 feet (61 m) of water after a short, fierce fight. French archaeologists discovered the wreck in 1984.

Divers have found many artifacts, including one of the ear-

*The Blakely rifle from the* Alabama

liest toilets, in the captain's cabin. Other artifacts from the ship's pantry and galley showed that the men aboard the raider lived well.

Divers also found and raised one of the ship's guns. One of the most modern and deadly weapons of the Civil War, it was known as a Blakely rifle. The gun was loaded, reminding the archaeologists that the *Alabama* sank in the middle of a battle. The *Alabama* was a well-built ship, modern for the time.

## The Submarine *H. L. Hunley*

The Civil War also saw the first successful submarine attack on a ship. Because submarines can sneak up on other ships, many navies have since eagerly adopted the submarine. The Confederate sub *H. L. Hunley* sank the USS *Housatonic* near Charleston, South Carolina.

During the Civil War, the Confederates also built underwater mines called torpedoes. These torpedoes sank the ironclad USS *Cairo* and sent the ironclad USS *Tecumseh* to the bottom with nearly all its crew.

Recently, archaeologists discovered the wreck of the submarine *H. L. Hunley*. After sinking the *Housatonic*, the *Hunley* disappeared into the dark night and the sea. It was never seen afloat again. The discovery of the *Hunley* buried in the sand near the wreck of the *Housatonic* solved a century-old mystery. Archaeologists are now making plans to raise the *Hunley* from the bottom. They have already learned that this early submarine was a carefully built and complicated piece of machinery. By the end of the Civil War in 1865, the U.S. Navy had learned much about new inventions and ways of building ships and guns.

*A 1863 painting of the submarine H. L. Hunley*

*The USS Massachusetts,*
*shown here in a*
*photograph from 1904,*
*was a U.S. Navy*
*battleship.*

# Chapter Seven

# The Rise of the Modern Navy

When the Civil War ended in 1865, Congress reduced the size of the navy. The few new ships that were built used lessons learned in the Civil War. These ships, which were made of steel and carried large guns, led the way to the modern battleship. Archaeologists have found some wrecks from this time.

Off the coast of North Carolina, archaeologists have studied the remains of the iron-hulled steam warship USS *Huron*. Built in 1875, the *Huron* was 175 feet (53 m) long and was one of the last navy ships built of iron. It was also one of the last navy ships that still had sails in case the engines failed. After the *Huron*, the navy began building ships of steel, which is stronger than iron.

During a bad storm in 1877, the *Huron* ran aground along a dangerous section of North Carolina coast. The heavy seas wrecked the ship and killed most of its 134 crew members. But the sea also buried sand around the ship. From time to time, winter storms strip away the sands, exposing the wreck. Archaeologists studying the *Huron* drew maps of the iron ship's hull and have recovered artifacts that include a pistol.

## An Early Battleship Wreck

In Florida, archaeologists have studied the wreck of one of the navy's earliest battleships, the USS *Massachusetts*. At 350 feet (107 m) long, the battleship was twice as long as the *Huron* and had a crew of 473. The USS *Massachusetts* entered naval service in 1896 and fought in World War I. After the war, the navy used the old battleship for target practice. After more than a hundred hits, the ship was left to sink slowly into Pensacola Bay.

Only one other U.S. navy ship from this time, the cruiser USS *Olympia*, still exists. All of the early battleships are gone.

# Launching Planes at Sea

The U.S. Navy built many more battleships after the *Massachusetts*. They made them bigger and bigger, with more powerful guns. They raced to build battleships faster than other countries could. Part of the naval arms race of the early twentieth century involved learning how to use aircraft to fight at sea.

In 1922, Billy Mitchell, a U.S. army general, used planes carrying bombs to sink a ship off the coast of Virginia. Mitchell's demonstration was one of many factors that persuaded the navy to get its own planes. The navy had already started to work with airplanes and built a ship to launch planes at sea.

# Dirigible Disasters

The U.S. Navy also experimented with airships, or **dirigibles**. These giant balloons carried planes and bombs. In the 1930s, the U.S. Navy built two giant dirigibles called the *Akron* and the *Macon*. The USS *Macon* was 735 feet (224 m) and sailed through the air instead of on the sea.

## The Ship That Billy Mitchell Sank

Divers have discovered the wreck of the ship that Billy Mitchell's bombers sank off the coast of Virginia. It was the German battleship *Ostfriesland*, captured and sent to the United States after Germany surrendered at the end of World War I.

*The dirigible called the* Macon *approaches an airfield in California.*

The *Macon* crashed into the sea off the coast of California and sank in 1935. In 1991, a robot-aided search near Monterey, California, discovered the broken metal frame of the *Macon* in nearly 1,400 feet (427 m) of water. Robots were used to photograph the underwater wreck.

The disaster of the *Macon* helped convince the navy not to use dirigibles for fighting. Instead, aircraft carriers—ships that carried planes on their decks—replaced battleships as the navy's most important ships. U.S. aircraft carriers played a big part in winning World War II.

*Flames and smoke pour from the USS Arizona in Pearl Harbor, Hawaii, after a surprise assault by the Japanese.*

# Chapter Eight

# World War II

In the 1930s, most of the world was at war. Japan invaded China. Many countries in Europe were fighting Germany. The United States stayed out of these wars. Some thought that war would spread to America, but most people felt safe since the wars across the ocean were a long way off.

Then Japan attacked the U.S. Navy base at Pearl Harbor, Hawaii, on December 7, 1941. Japanese planes launched from aircraft carriers bombed American vessels anchored in the harbor. Many ships were sunk and thousands died. The United States declared war on Japan,

## Underwater Robots

Robots carrying cameras and scientific instruments plung deep in the ocean to depths far below where humans can safely dive. These robots have explored deep-sea volcanoes and shipwrecks such as the *Titanic*. They are operated by remote control from a control station on the water's surface. These valuable pieces of equipment are called remotely operated vehicles, or ROVs.

and Germany declared war on the United States. During the war, the U.S. Navy grew. At the end of the war in 1945, it was the most powerful navy in the world.

Hundreds of U.S. warships were lost during many World War II battles. Archaeologists have dived on some of them, including the ships at Pearl Harbor. They have used robots to explore ships lost in battle near the South Pacific island of Guadalcanal.

# Underwater Graves

Most of the ships sunk at Pearl Harbor were raised from the bottom. But two battleships, the USS *Arizona* and the USS *Utah*, were too badly damaged to move and remained where they sank. Both are war graves. On the *Arizona*, 1,177 U.S. sailors and marines were killed. Archaeologists dived on the battleship. But they did not go inside, out of respect for the dead.

The archaeologists found that many bombs hit the *Arizona*. Men were fighting several fires onboard with hoses when a big bomb dropped on the ship and punched through the steel deck. It exploded in an area where explosives were kept. The ship blew up in a huge ball of fire. Divers found fire hoses on the deck, where the sailors had dropped them when they died.

The archaeologists drew a map of the *Arizona* to show how the ship blew up. The steel hull and decks were torn open and bent out. It looks like a giant fist punched through the front of the ship. A huge turret, with its guns bent down, lies inside the hull. But many of the glass portholes on the side of the ship are not broken.

Remotely operated vehicles have dived on the wrecks of the warships sunk at Guadalcanal, where the United States and Japan fought at sea. Most of the wrecks are in water more than 1,000 feet (305 m) deep. Using the robot cameras, archaeologists have learned about how the ships sank.

World War II ended in August 1945 when the United States dropped two atomic bombs on Japan. The atomic bomb

## The Bottom of the Sea

The sea battles off Guadalcanal sank so many ships that the area is called Ironbottom Sound.

changed how people thought about war. Some people thought that armies and navies were no longer necessary.

## Navy Power

In July 1946, on Bikini island in the middle of the Pacific Ocean, the United States tested the atomic bomb against ships, guns, and tanks. More than twenty ships were sunk, including battleships, submarines, destroyers, and an aircraft carrier. The power of two bombs sank them all in seconds. Archaeologists have dived on the wrecks at Bikini and were amazed to see that the heat of the bombs had melted steel.

The United States still has the world's most powerful navy. Hundreds of U.S. warships sail the oceans. These ships are armed with powerful new weapons, including missiles and atomic bombs. Jets fly off aircraft carriers at supersonic speeds. Submarines dive deep in the ocean and stay down for weeks. Sometimes these ships, planes, and missiles are lost. In the future, archaeologists may dive on and study them. Who knows what they will learn?

*The 1946 atomic bomb test at Bikini in the Pacific Ocean*

# Glossary

**archaeologist**—a scientist who studies past cultures based on artifacts and other evidence left behind

**artifacts**—the things people make that show human work

**baseline**—the line from which all other measurements start on a map

**brig**—a square-rigged sailing ship with two masts

**clipper**—a fast-sailing ship with tall masts and large sails

**cofferdam**—a watertight enclosure used to make underwater repairs of a ship

**dirigibles**—airships that carry planes and bombs

**dredge**—a machine for removing sand or mud

**excavate**—to scientifically recover and study the remains of past human activity

**expedition**—a journey for a specific purpose

**fascines**—large bundles of twigs and saplings tied together along the sides of a boat for protection

**flotilla**—a small fleet or group of vessels

**frigate**—a square-rigged warship

**gondola**—a flat-bottomed cargo boat

**gunboat**—a flat-bottomed rowboat that had a mast and a sail and carried cannons

**hull**—the frame or body of a ship

**ironclads**—wooden ships covered with armor

**magazine**—the place where a ship's gunpowder was stored

**men-of-war**—warships

**pilfer**—to steal things of small value or in small amounts

**privateers**—vessels that were owned by private citizens and preyed on unarmed enemy merchant ships

**raiders**—fast steam-powered warships that attacked merchant ships

**salvage**—to recover or save, especially from wreckage

**stern**—the back or rear end of a ship

**submarines**—naval ships that move and operate underwater

**teredos**—undersea worms

**turret**—a warship's revolving round tower that protects guns mounted in it

# To Find Out More

## Books

Blashfield, Jean F. *Blockade Runners and Ironclads: Naval Action in the Civil War*. Danbury, Conn.: Franklin Watts, 1997.

Carter, Alden R. *Battle of the Ironclads: The Monitor and the Merrimack*. Danbury, Conn.: Franklin Watts, 1993.

Dolan, Edward F. *The American Revolution: How We Fought the War of Independence*. Brookfield, Conn.: Millbrook Press, 1995.

Naden, Corinne. *The U.S. Navy*. Brookfield, Conn.: Millbrook Press, 1992.

Schultz, Ron. *Looking Inside Sunken Treasure*. Sante Fe, N. Mex.: John Muir, 1993.

Stein, R. Conrad. *The USS Arizona*. Danbury, Conn.: Children's Press, 1992.

Taylor, Theodore, and W. T. Mars (illustrator). *Air-Raid—Pearl Harbor! The Story of December 7, 1941.* New York: Harcourt, 1991.

# Organizations and Online Sites

Historic Naval Ships Association of North America
4640 Hoylake Drive
Virginia Beach, VA 23462
*http://www.maritime.org/hnsa-guide.htm*
This national association represents all the warships preserved as public museums or memorials.

Maine State Museum
83 State House Station
Augusta, ME 04333
*http://www.mainemuseums.org/htm/54.htm*
This museum displays many artifacts from the *Defence.*

National Museum of American History
Smithsonian Institution
14th Street and Constitution Avenue NW
Washington, DC 20560
*http://www.si.edu/nmah/index.htm*
This museum displays the entire hull and artifacts of the gunboat *Philadelphia.*

National Oceanic and Atmospheric Administration (NOAA)
1305 East West Highway
Silver Spring, MD 20910
*http://www.nos.noaa.gov/*
This website offers details about the famous ironclad *Monitor*.

Naval Historical Center
Washington Navy Yard
805 Kidder Dreese SE
Washington, DC 20374
*http://www.history.navy.mil/*
This U.S. Navy center provides information about the *Tecumseh* and the Confederate raider *Alabama*.

South Carolina Institute of Anthropology and Archaeology
1321 Pendleton Street
Columbia, SC 29208
*http://www.cla.sc.edu/sciaa/hunley1.html*
This website has details about the *H. L. Hunley*.

U.S. National Park Service
Submerged Cultural Resources Unit
P.O. Box 728
Santa Fe, NM 87501
*http://www.nps.gov/scru.htm*
This website has links to pages about the USS *Arizona*, the USS *Utah*, and the Bikini wrecks.

# A Note on Sources

Like most authors, I have my own way of researching when I write a book. I usually start in the library. I also check scientific journals and popular magazines for related articles. *Archaeology* magazine, published by the Archaeological Institute of America, was particularly useful. This publication is also online at *www.archaeology.org*. This organization has a new magazine just for kids called *Dig!*

I also talked to other archaeologists who work around the world on shipwrecks and other sites. They offered hints, gave suggestions of people to speak with, and directed me to Internet sites. Most of the archaeologists I know are always willing to answer questions and help other researchers and students.

—*James P. Delgado*

# Index

Numbers in *italics* indicate illustrations.

aircraft carriers, 47, *52*
airships. *See* dirigibles.
American Revolution. *See* Revolutionary War.
archaeology, 7, 10, 15, 19, 21–22, *23*, 33, 35, 51. *See also* artifacts.
Arnold, Benedict, 14, *14*
artifacts, 16, 38. *See also* archaeology.
  CSS *Alabama*, *39, 40*
  *Defence* (brig), *23*, 24–25, *24, 25*
  *Philadelphia* (man-of-war), *16*
  USS *Huron*, 44
  USS *Scorpion*, 29, *30*
atomic testing, 6, *52, 52–53*

Barney, Joshua, 28
baselines, 33, 35

Battle of Lexington, *12*
battleships, 44
Bikini island, 6, 52, *52–53*
Blakely rifles, 39–40, *39*
British Royal Navy, 19–20

Chesapeake flotilla, 28
Civil War, 37–38, 43
clipper ships, 33
CSS *Alabama*, *8*, 39
CSS *H. L. Hunley*, 10, *10–11*, 40–41, *41*
CSS *Virginia*, 37

*Defence* (brig), 20–22, *21*
dirigibles, 45

fascines, 15–17
food, 22, 24

Guadalcanal, 51–52

gunboats, 13–14

Hamilton, Thomas, 29

Ironbottom Sound, 52
ironclads, 37

Lake Champlain, 14
Lake Champlain Maritime
    Museum, 17
Lake Ontario, 30
lakes, 9

Maine Maritime Academy,
    20
maps
    *Defence*, 21–22, *21*
    USS *Scorpion*, 29
men-of-war, 7, *16*, *18*
Mitchell, Billy, 45
USS *Monitor* (ironclad), *36*,
    37–38
mutiny, 32

oceans, 9–10
"Old Ironsides." *See* USS
    *Constitution*.

Pearl Harbor, *4–5*, 5, 6–7,
    *48*, 49–50

Penobscot expedition,
    19–20, 25
Penobscot River, 20
*Philadelphia* (gunboat),
    13–17, *15*
*Philadelphia II*, *17*
privateers, 19–20

raiders (warships), 38–39
remotely operated vehicles
    (ROVs), 47, 50–51, *50*
Revolutionary War, 13, 15,
    19–20
rivers, 9

"salt horse" (food), 22, 24
Semmes, Raphael, 33
Spencer, Philip, 31
submarines, 10, 40, 52

U.S. Navy, 13–14, 27–28,
    37, 43, 45, 49
USS *Akron* (dirgible), 45
USS *Arizona*, 6, 10, *48*, 51
USS *Arizona* Memorial, *4–5*,
    5–6
USS *Cairo*, 41
USS *Constitution*, 10, *26*, 28
USS *Hamilton*, 30
USS *Housatonic*, 40

USS *Huron*, 44
USS *Kearsarge*, 39
USS *Macon*, 45–47, *46–47*
USS *Massachusetts*, *42–43*, 44
USS *Monitor*, 6–7, 38
USS *Olympia*, 44
USS *Scorpion*, 28–30, *29*
USS *Scourge*, 30
USS *Somers* (brig), *6*, 30,
    31–33, *32, 34–35*, 35
USS *Tecumseh*, 41

USS *Utah*, 51

Veracruz, 32, *32*

War of 1812, *26*, 28, 30–31
warships, 10, 13, 30, 39,
    50, *52*
Wentworth, Caesar, 29
World War I, *44*
World War II, 5, 7, 47, *48*,
    50

# About the Author

James P. Delgado has worked as a park ranger, a historian, an underwater archaeologist, a teacher, and a museum director. His love of archaeology began when he was ten, and he went on his first dig at age fourteen. Today, he is the executive director of Vancouver Maritime Museum.

James P. Delgado has written eighteen books related to history and underwater archaeology. He is also the author of the Watts Library books *Native American Shipwrecks* and *Shipwrecks from the Westward Movement*. He currently lives in Vancouver, British Columbia.